Can you break the CODE?

CODE BREAKER

USE THE CODES BELOW TO HELP ANSWER THE CODE BREAKER QUESTIONS WITHIN THE WORKBOOK

CONTENTS

1 | Revelation of Surah Al Kahf 03
2 | Status of the Prophet ﷺ 06
3 | Making Dua 09
4 | Going into the Cave 12
5 | Sleeping in the Cave 15
6 | Protection from Jahanum 18
7 | The Two Gardens 21
8 | Creation of Adam 24
9 | Thanking Allah 27
10 | The Quran 30
11 | Being Humble 33
12 | Mercy of Allah 36
13 | Finding Khidr 39
14 | Saying InshaAllah 42
15 | Story of Khidr 45
16 | Story of the Orphans 48
17 | Story of Dhul Qarnayn 51
18 | Yajuj and Majuj 54
19 | End of Yajuj and Majuj 57
20 | The Ka'bah 60

Reward Chart

Dearest viewers, welcome to your new workbook!

There are 20 worksheets to complete, you can find the answers for the worksheets based on every episode of The Azharis. Each worksheet will help you learn more about Surah Al Kahf. Once you have completed the worksheet choose the matching sticker from the sticker page and stick it in correctly after each episode or if you prefer colour it in.

DON'T FORGET TO FOLLOW US!

@theazharisofficial

Episode 1   Episode 2   Episode 3   Episode 4   Episode 5

Episode 6   Episode 7   Episode 8   Episode 9   Episode 10

Episode 11   Episode 12   Episode 13   Episode 14   Episode 15

Episode 16   Episode 17   Episode 18   Episode 19   Episode 20

Revelation of Surah Al Kahf

Verse 1

1- Where was this Surah revealed?
Break the code | Refer to the code breaker sheet

__ __ __ __ __

2- How many memorised verses will protect you from Dajjal?
Colour the correct answer

3- Complete the hadith:

Fill in the correct answer

"The best deeds are those done .... even if they are small." [Ibn Majah]

4- Word Puzzle

Colour in the stars as you write the words in the boxes

☆ Allah

☆ Mecca

☆ Quran

☆ Kahf

☆ Friday

5- Quranic Arabic

Trace the Arabic word and join the dots

All Praise belongs to Allah

ٱلْحَمْدُ لِلَّهِ ٱلَّذِىٓ أَنزَلَ عَلَىٰ عَبْدِهِ ٱلْكِتَٰبَ وَلَمْ يَجْعَل لَّهُۥ عِوَجَا

[Verse : 1]

COMPETITION TIME!

Watch the 1st episode for the questions

Circle the correct answer

Each correct answer is worth 2 points, leaving you with a total score out of 6

Let's see if you can beat The Azharis!

Question	Answer (Circle the correct answer)		Score
1	Four	Two	
2	Musa عليه السلام	Dawud عليه السلام	
3	Ikhlas	Kawthar	
TOTAL SCORE			

THE AZHARI PAD

Watch episode 1 for the question

SURAH AL KAHF   PAGE 5   EPISODE - 1

Status of the Prophet ﷺ

Verse 1 - 2

1- The Quran will guide us to?
Find your way to the correct answer

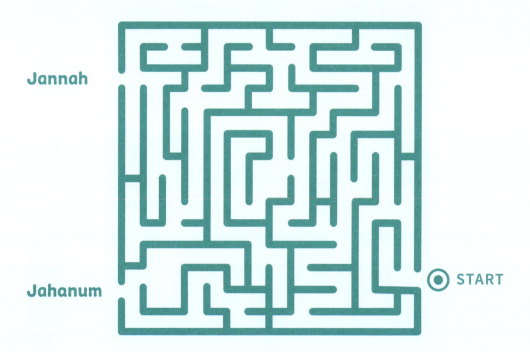

2- The key to our place in Jannah is our good deeds.
Circle the correct answer

TRUE - FALSE

3- What does the word عبد ABD in verse one mean?

Colour in

Slave

4- Wordsearch

Tick off the words as you find them

J	S	A	L	L	A	H
A	B	L	Q	O	P	E
N	E	R	A	G	D	X
N	S	O	K	V	V	M
A	R	H	O	A	E	L
H	E	N	T	D	H	W
I	V	L	I	O	N	F

☆ Allah
☆ Jannah
☆ Slave
☆ Kahf
☆ Verse

5- Quranic Arabic

Trace the the Arabic word and join the dots

Ajr

Reward

قَيِّمًا لِّيُنذِرَ بَأْسًا شَدِيدًا مِّن لَّدُنْهُ وَيُبَشِّرَ ٱلْمُؤْمِنِينَ ٱلَّذِينَ يَعْمَلُونَ ٱلصَّٰلِحَٰتِ أَنَّ لَهُمْ أَجْرًا حَسَنًا

[Verse : 2]

COMPETITION TIME!

Watch the 2nd episode for the questions

Circle the correct answer

Each correct answer is worth 2 points, leaving you with a total score out of 6

Let's see if you can beat The Azharis!

Question	Answer (Circle the correct answer)		Score
1	Left	Right	
2	Eesa عليه السلام	Musa عليه السلام	
3	Sheep	Camel	
TOTAL SCORE			

THE AZHARI PAD

Watch episode 2 for the question

SURAH AL KAHF — PAGE 8 — EPISODE - 2

Making Dua

Verse 3 - 10

1- Caring about the environment is part of being Muslim.
Colour the correct answer

2- What were the people in the cave first doing?
Write your answer below and join the dots

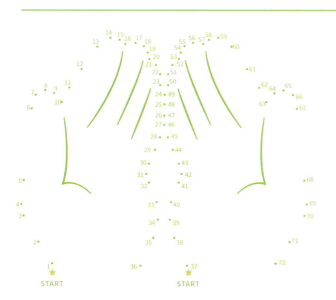

3- The Prophet ﷺ wanted good for all no matter who they were?

Join the dots of the correct answer

4- Doing things to the best of your ability is called?

Break the code | Refer to the code breaker sheet

___ ___ ___ ___ ___

5- Quranic Arabic

Trace the Arabic word and join the dots

Ard

Earth

[Verse : 7]

SURAH AL KAHF   PAGE 10   EPISODE - 3

COMPETITION TIME!

Watch the 3rd episode for the questions

Circle the correct answer

Each correct answer is worth 2 points, leaving you with a total score out of 6

Let's see if you can beat The Azharis!

Question	Answer (Circle the correct answer)		Score
1	Mecca	Medinah	
2	Nuh عليه السلام	Sulaiman عليه السلام	
3	Face	Feet	
TOTAL SCORE			

THE AZHARI PAD

Watch episode 3 for the question

SURAH AL KAHF　　　PAGE 11　　　EPISODE - 3

Going into the cave

Verse 11 - 14

1- Which body part was mentioned in verse 11?
   Colour the correct answer

HAND - EAR

2- How long did the people of the cave sleep for?
   Find your way to the correct answer

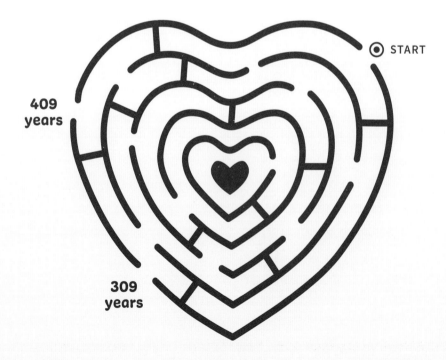

3- Why did they go to the cave?

Write the answer below

_____

_____

4- We can get the mercy of Allah by being merciful...

Break the code | Refer to the code breaker sheet

__ __   __ __ __ __ __ __

5- Quranic Arabic

Trace the Arabic word and join the dots

وَرَبَطْنَا عَلَىٰ قُلُوبِهِمْ إِذْ قَامُوا۟ فَقَالُوا۟ رَبُّنَا رَبُّ ٱلسَّمَٰوَٰتِ وَٱلْأَرْضِ لَن نَّدْعُوَا۟ مِن دُونِهِۦٓ إِلَٰهًا ۖ لَّقَدْ قُلْنَآ إِذًا شَطَطًا

Heart

[Verse : 14]

SURAH AL KAHF — PAGE 13 — EPISODE - 4

COMPETITION TIME!

Watch the 4th episode for the questions

Circle the correct answer

Each correct answer is worth 2 points, leaving you with a total score out of 6

Let's see if you can beat The Azharis!

Question	Answer (Circle the correct answer)		Score
1	Bread	Dates	
2	Mecca	Medinah	
3	Left	Right	
TOTAL SCORE			

THE AZHARI PAD

Watch episode 4 for the question

SURAH AL KAHF — PAGE 14 — EPISODE - 4

Sleeping in the cave

Verse 15 - 21

1- Why weren't the people in the cave harmed by the sun?
Underline the correct answer

It was not sunny

Allah turned them

It was raining

2- What did the shopkeeper think the money was?
Unscamble the letters

R U E R A T S E

3- What type of food did they ask for?
   Colour the correct answer

Healthy - Unhealthy

4- Wordsearch
   Tick off the words as you find them

   ☆ Cave
   ☆ Money
   ☆ Sun
   ☆ Shade
   ☆ Rain
   ☆ Move

S	M	A	R	O	R	J
A	O	O	W	N	A	A
L	V	J	N	K	I	E
P	E	G	D	E	N	V
B	J	N	E	A	Y	A
H	U	E	A	L	H	C
S	H	A	D	E	T	Z

5- Quranic Arabic
   Trace the Arabic word and join the dots

Rahma

Mercy

وَإِذِ ٱعْتَزَلْتُمُوهُمْ وَمَا يَعْبُدُونَ إِلَّا ٱللَّهَ فَأْوُۥٓا۟ إِلَى ٱلْكَهْفِ يَنشُرْ لَكُمْ رَبُّكُم مِّن رَّحْمَتِهِۦ وَيُهَيِّئْ لَكُم مِّنْ أَمْرِكُم مِّرْفَقًا

[Verse : 16]

SURAH AL KAHF   PAGE 16   EPISODE - 5

COMPETITION TIME!

Watch the 5th episode for the questions

Circle the correct answer

Each correct answer is worth 2 points, leaving you with a total score out of 6

Let's see if you can beat The Azharis!

Question	Answer (Circle the correct answer)		Score
1	Iftar	Suhur	
2	Fatiha	Baqarah	
3	40	50	

TOTAL SCORE

THE AZHARI PAD

Watch episode 5 for the question

SURAH AL KAHF — PAGE 17 — EPISODE - 5

Protection from Jahanum

Verse 22 - 31

1- Which animal was outside of the cave?
Join the dots of the correct answer

2- How can we protect ourselves from Jahanum?
Colour in

Allahumma inni authubika min adhabi jahanum
[Bukhari]

3- How many rivers are in Jannah?

Find your way to the correct answer

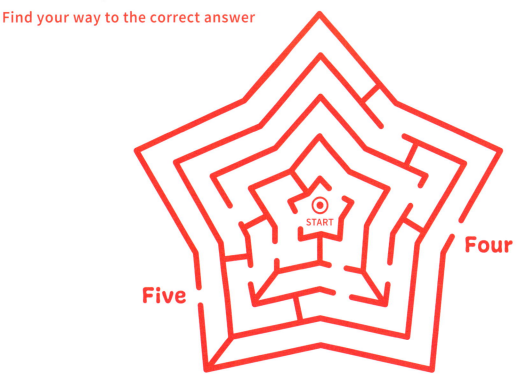

4- How many people were in the cave?

Tick the correct answer

☐ 7   ☐ 10   ☐ 15

5- Quranic Arabic

Trace the Arabic word and join the dots

Sabr

Patience

وَٱصْبِرْ نَفْسَكَ مَعَ ٱلَّذِينَ يَدْعُونَ رَبَّهُم بِٱلْغَدَوٰةِ وَٱلْعَشِيِّ يُرِيدُونَ وَجْهَهُ

[Verse : 28]

COMPETITION TIME!

Watch the 6st episode for the questions

Circle the correct answer

Each correct answer is worth 2 points, leaving you with a total score out of 6

Let's see if you can beat The Azharis!

Question	Answer (Circle the correct answer)		Score
1	Zakah	Hajj	
2	Subhanallah	Alhamdulillah	
3	Medinah	Mecca	
TOTAL SCORE			

THE AZHARI PAD

Watch episode 6 for the question

SURAH AL KAHF — PAGE 20 — EPISODE - 6

The two gardens

Verse 32 - 35

1- Who was tested in the story of the two gardens?
Underline the correct answer

The rich man

The poor man

Both

2- How can we increase our wealth?
Break the code | Refer to the code breaker sheet

___ ___ ___ ___ ___ ___ ___ ___

___ ___ ___ ___ ___

3- What dua should we recite after praying?

Colour in

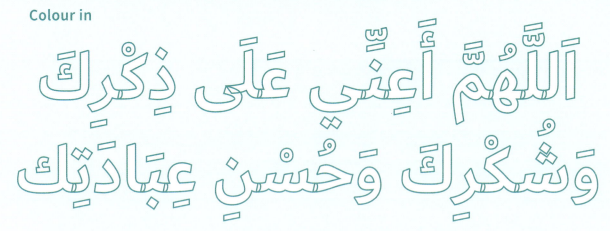

Allahumma a-inni ala dhikrika, wa shukrika, wa husni ibadatik
[Bukhari]

4- Word Puzzle

Colour in the stars as you write the words in the boxes

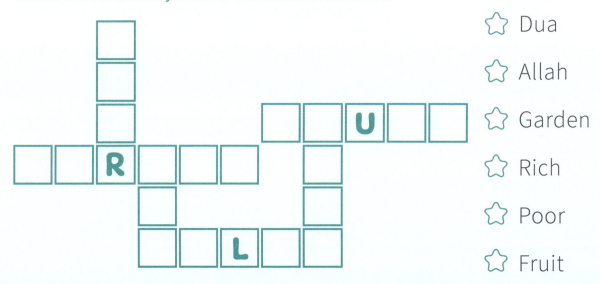

☆ Dua
☆ Allah
☆ Garden
☆ Rich
☆ Poor
☆ Fruit

5- Quranic Arabic

Trace the Arabic word and join the dots

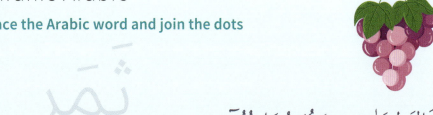

ثَمَر

Thamar

Fruit

وَكَانَ لَهُۥ ثَمَرٌ فَقَالَ لِصَـٰحِبِهِۦ وَهُوَ يُحَاوِرُهُۥٓ أَنَا۠ أَكْثَرُ مِنكَ مَالًا وَأَعَزُّ نَفَرًا

[Verse : 34]

SURAH AL KAHF — PAGE 22 — EPISODE - 7

COMPETITION TIME!

Watch the 7th episode for the questions

Circle the correct answer

Each correct answer is worth 2 points, leaving you with a total score out of 6

Let's see if you can beat The Azharis!

Question	Answer (Circle the correct answer)		Score
1	Jibril	Israfil	
2	Three	Four	
3	Abu Bakr رضي الله عنه	Bilal رضي الله عنه	

TOTAL SCORE

THE AZHARI PAD

Watch episode 7 for the question

SURAH AL KAHF — PAGE 23 — EPISODE - 7

Creation of Adam
عليه السلام

Verse 36 - 41

1- What does sa'at ساعة refer to?
   Underline the correct answer

   Short Time - Long Time - Middle Time

2- What did Allah create Adam عليه السلام from?
   Find your way to the answer

3- When we see something good what should we say?

Write the answer below

4- Does having more money mean Allah loves us more?

Circle the correct answer

TRUE | FALSE

5- Quranic Arabic

Trace the Arabic word and join the dots

Maal

Money

أَنَا أَقَلَّ مِنكَ مَالًا وَوَلَدًا

[Verse : 39]

COMPETITION TIME!

Watch the 8th episode for the questions

Circle the correct answer

Each correct answer is worth 2 points, leaving you with a total score out of 6

Let's see if you can beat The Azharis!

Question	Answer (Circle the correct answer)		Score
1	Suhur	Iftar	
2	Left	Right	
3	Medinah	Mecca	
TOTAL SCORE			

THE AZHARI PAD

Watch episode 8 for the question

SURAH AL KAHF — PAGE 26 — EPISODE - 8

Thanking Allah

Verse 42 - 44

1- Did the rich man thank Allah for his garden?

Choose the correct answer

Yes - No

2- Wordsearch

Tick off the words as you find them

T	E	A	R	I	C	H
H	P	S	M	A	L	L
A	B	I	G	E	D	N
N	O	N	O	I	L	N
K	J	V	O	X	H	A
D	E	E	D	T	C	H
I	Z	L	N	A	T	E

☆ Thank
☆ Deed
☆ Good
☆ Big
☆ Small
☆ Rich

3- The reward of a small deed can be made big if your

_____ is good.

Fill in the gap with the correct answer

4- What happened to the rich person's garden?
Tick the correct answer

☐ **Increased**

☐ **Destroyed**

☐ **Had more trees given**

5- Quranic Arabic
Trace the Arabic word and join the dots

Haq

Truth

هُنَالِكَ ٱلْوَلَيَةُ لِلَّهِ ٱلْحَقِّ
هُوَ خَيْرٌ ثَوَابًا وَخَيْرٌ عُقْبًا

[Verse : 44]

COMPETITION TIME!

Watch the 9th episode for the questions

Circle the correct answer

Each correct answer is worth 2 points, leaving you with a total score out of 6

Let's see if you can beat The Azharis!

Question	Answer (Circle the correct answer)		Score
1	Abdullah	Ilyas	
2	Israfil	Jibril	
3	Yes	No	
TOTAL SCORE			

THE AZHARI PAD

Watch episode 9 for the question

SURAH AL KAHF — PAGE 29 — EPISODE - 9

The Quran

Verse 45 - 49

DON'T FORGET!

Download your achievement certificate after completing 10 epsiodes from www.theazharis.com

1- What was the example mentioned that comes down from the sky like the Quran came down?

Break the code | Refer to the code breaker sheet

___ ___ ___ ___

2- What should be recited before bed?

Trace in Arabic

x 33 Times   x 33 Times

x 34 Times

SURAH AL KAHF   PAGE 30   EPISODE - 10

3- What hand will good people receive their books in on the day of judgement?

Colour in the correct hand

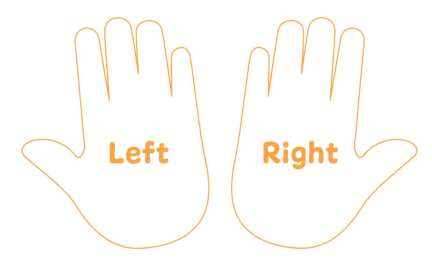

4- We will all be lined up in rows on the day of judgement?

Tick the correct answer

◯ True

◯ False

5- Quranic Arabic

Trace the Arabic word and join the dots

Anzal

To descend

وَٱضْرِبْ لَهُم مَّثَلَ ٱلْحَيَوٰةِ ٱلدُّنْيَا كَمَآءٍ أَنزَلْنَٰهُ مِنَ ٱلسَّمَآءِ فَٱخْتَلَطَ بِهِۦ نَبَاتُ ٱلْأَرْضِ فَأَصْبَحَ هَشِيمًا تَذْرُوهُ ٱلرِّيَٰحُ

[Verse : 45]

COMPETITION TIME!

Watch the 10th episode for the questions

Circle the correct answer

Each correct answer is worth 2 points, leaving you with a total score out of 6

Let's see if you can beat The Azharis!

Question	Answer (Circle the correct answer)		Score
1	Right	Left	
2	Ismail عليه السلام	Ibrahim عليه السلام	
3	Adhan	Iqamah	
TOTAL SCORE			

THE AZHARI PAD

Watch episode 10 for the question

SURAH AL KAHF — PAGE 32 — EPISODE - 10

Being Humble

Verse 50 - 57

1- Does Allah favour certain colours of skin over others?
   Trace the correct answer

2- How many ropes hold Jahanum?
   Circle the correct answer

700

7000

70000

3- The dua to help learning is:

Colour in

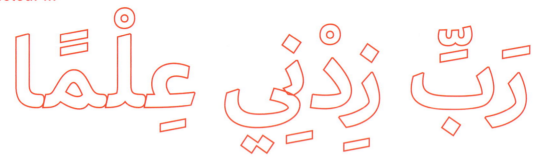

Rabbi Zidni Ilma
[Surah Taha : 114]

4- Word Puzzle

Colour in the stars as you write the words in the boxes

☆ Allah
☆ Learn
☆ Jahanum
☆ Rope
☆ Colour

5- Quranic Arabic

Trace the Arabic word and join the dots

Nas

People

وَلَقَدْ صَرَّفْنَا فِى هَٰذَا ٱلْقُرْءَانِ لِلنَّاسِ مِن كُلِّ مَثَلٍ ۚ وَكَانَ ٱلْإِنسَٰنُ أَكْثَرَ شَىْءٍ جَدَلًا

[Verse : 54]

SURAH AL KAHF   PAGE 34   EPISODE - 11

COMPETITION TIME!

Watch the 11th episode for the questions

Circle the correct answer

Each correct answer is worth 2 points, leaving you with a total score out of 6

Let's see if you can beat The Azharis!

Question	Answer (Circle the correct answer)		Score
1	Hawa عليها السلام	Hajar عليها السلام	
2	Tarawih	Duha	
3	Surah Al Kahf	Surah Al Mulk	
TOTAL SCORE			

THE AZHARI PAD

Watch episode 11 for the question

SURAH AL KAHF — PAGE 35 — EPISODE - 11

Mercy of Allah

Verse 58 - 60

1- Out of Allah's mercy he punishes us straight away?
Write True or False

2- What was the name of the boy that went with Musa عليه السلام?
Find your way to the answer

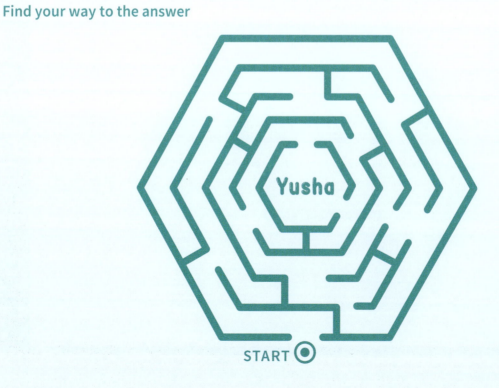

3- The best people, are those who constantly

Complete the Hadith

....

[Tirmidhi]

4- What animal did Musa عليه السلام have in his basket?

Join the dots and write the answer

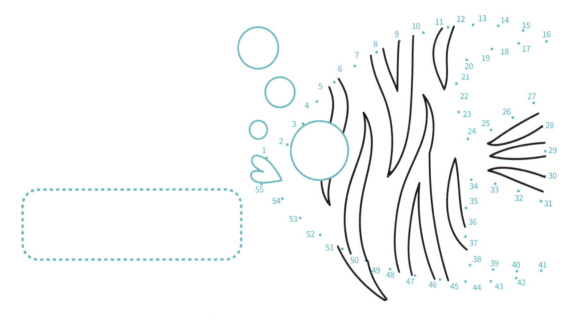

5- Quranic Arabic

Trace the Arabic word and join the dots

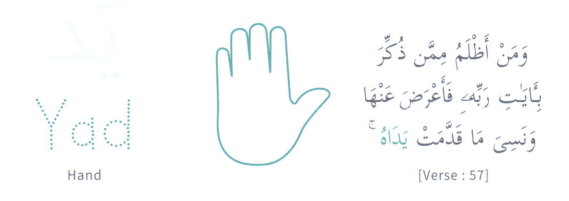

Yad

Hand

[Verse : 57]

COMPETITION TIME!

Watch the 12th episode for the questions

Circle the correct answer

Each correct answer is worth 2 points, leaving you with a total score out of 6

Let's see if you can beat The Azharis!

Question	Answer (Circle the correct answer)		Score
1	Three	Four	
2	Shepherds	Fishermen	
3	Firawn	Abu Jahl	
TOTAL SCORE			

THE AZHARI PAD

Watch episode 12 for the question

SURAH AL KAHF

Finding Khidr

Verse 61 - 67

1- Who forgot about the fish?
Circle the correct answer

Musa or Yusha

2- Before we start reciting Quran what do we say?
Colour in

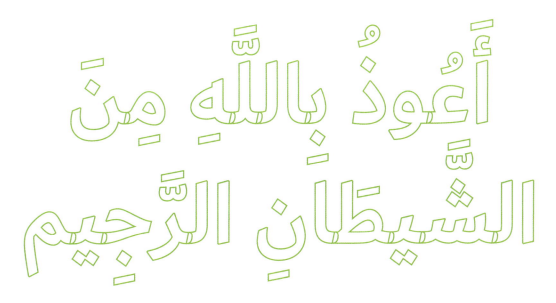

Audhu billahi minash shaitanir rajeem
[Surah An-Nahl : 98]

3- What was the name of the man they found?
Circle the correct answer

Musa - Khidr - Yunus

4- What colour did the land turn wherever he went?
Break the code | Refer to the code breaker sheet

___ ___ ___ ___ ___

5- Quranic Arabic
Trace the Arabic word and join the dots

Nasiya

To forget

قَالَ أَرَءَيْتَ إِذْ أَوَيْنَا إِلَى ٱلصَّخْرَةِ فَإِنِّى نَسِيتُ ٱلْحُوتَ وَمَا أَنسَىٰنِيهُ إِلَّا ٱلشَّيْطَٰنُ أَنْ أَذْكُرَهُ

[Verse : 63]

COMPETITION TIME!

Watch the 13th episode for the questions

Circle the correct answer

Each correct answer is worth 2 points, leaving you with a total score out of 6

Let's see if you can beat The Azharis!

Question	Answer		Score
	(Circle the correct answer)		
1	Left	Right	
2	Charity	Penalty	
3	Yaqub عليه السلام	Yusuf عليه السلام	
TOTAL SCORE			

THE AZHARI PAD

Watch episode 13 for the question

SURAH AL KAHF — PAGE 41 — EPISODE - 13

Saying InshaAllah

Verse 68 -73

1- What did Khidr say Musa عليه السلام wouldn't have?
Break the code | Refer to the code breaker sheet

___ ___ ___ ___ ___ ___ ___ ___ ___

2- If we want to do something what should we say before?
Join the dots

3- What did Musa عليه السلام and Khidr go onto?
   Draw and write the answer

4- What did Musa عليه السلام forget?
   Underline the correct answer

   Not to ask questions

   Ask questions

5- Quranic Arabic
   Trace the Arabic word and join the dots

Safeenah
Boat

فَٱنطَلَقَا حَتَّىٰٓ إِذَا رَكِبَا فِى ٱلسَّفِينَةِ خَرَقَهَا

[Verse : 71]

COMPETITION TIME!

Watch the 14th episode for the questions

Circle the correct answer

Each correct answer is worth 2 points, leaving you with a total score out of 6

Let's see if you can beat The Azharis!

Question	Answer (Circle the correct answer)		Score
1	Aminah رضي الله عنها	Safiyah رضي الله عنها	
2	63	73	
3	Eesa عليه السلام	Muhammad صلى الله عليه وسلم	
TOTAL SCORE			

THE AZHARI PAD

Watch episode 14 for the question

SURAH AL KAHF — EPISODE - 14

Story of Khidr

Verse 74 - 79

1- Which Prophet used a slingshot?

Break the code | Refer to the code breaker sheet

___ ___ ___ ___ ___ ___

2- Why did the King not take the boat?

Write the answer below

_____

3- Did the people of the town give Musa & Khidr food?

Colour the correct answer

4- What did Khidr do to the wall that was falling down?

Trace the letters

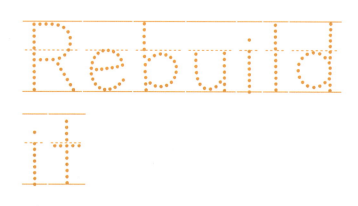

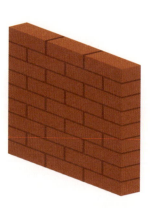

5- Quranic Arabic

Trace the Arabic word and join the dots

King

وَكَانَ وَرَآءَهُم مَّلِكٌ
يَأْخُذُ كُلَّ سَفِينَةٍ غَصْبًا

[Verse : 79]

SURAH AL KAHF   PAGE 46   EPISODE - 15

COMPETITION TIME!

Watch the 15th episode for the questions

Circle the correct answer

Each correct answer is worth 2 points, leaving you with a total score out of 6

Let's see if you can beat The Azharis!

Question	Answer (Circle the correct answer)		Score
1	Ibrahim عليه السلام	Ishaq عليه السلام	
2	Medinah	Masjid Al Aqsa	
3	Haman	Harun عليه السلام	
TOTAL SCORE			

THE AZHARI PAD

Watch episode 15 for the question

SURAH AL KAHF — PAGE 47 — EPISODE - 15

Story of the Orphans

Verse 80 - 92

1- Who did the wall belong to?
   Circle the correct answer

Orphans   **Workers**

Businessmen

2- What does Dhul Qarnayn mean?
   Trace the correct answer

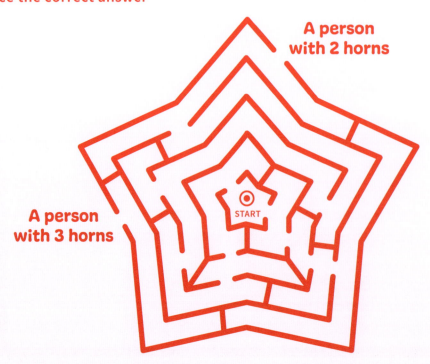

SURAH AL KAHF — PAGE 48 — EPISODE - 16

3- What was buried under the wall?

Write the answer below

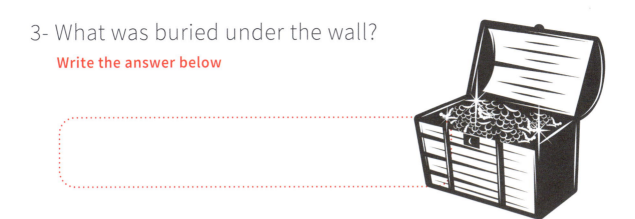

4- Word Puzzle

Colour in the stars as you write the words in the boxes

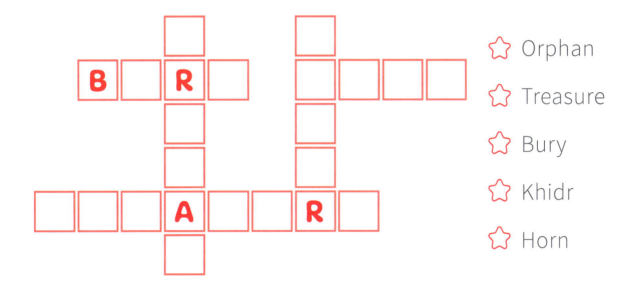

☆ Orphan

☆ Treasure

☆ Bury

☆ Khidr

☆ Horn

5- Quranic Arabic

Trace the Arabic word and join the dots

Good

فَأَرَدْنَآ أَن يُبْدِلَهُمَا رَبُّهُمَا خَيْرًا مِّنْهُ زَكَوٰةً وَأَقْرَبَ رُحْمًا

[Verse : 81]

SURAH AL KAHF   PAGE 49   EPISODE - 16

COMPETITION TIME!

Watch the 16th episode for the questions

Circle the correct answer

Each correct answer is worth 2 points, leaving you with a total score out of 6

Let's see if you can beat The Azharis!

Question	Answer (Circle the correct answer)		Score
1	Khalid رضي الله عنه	Zayd رضي الله عنه	
2	Abu Bakr رضي الله عنه	Uthman رضي الله عنه	
3	Nuh عليه السلام	Musa عليه السلام	
TOTAL SCORE			

THE AZHARI PAD

Watch episode 16 for the question

SURAH AL KAHF — PAGE 50 — EPISODE - 16

Story of Dhul Qarnayn

Verse 87 - 93

1- Was Dhul Qarnayn a good person?
Colour the correct answer

2- Wordsearch
Tick off the words as you find them

J	E	A	R	A	W	P
H	S	C	A	L	E	R
Y	A	I	G	L	D	O
U	F	D	X	A	L	P
S	J	V	I	H	Q	H
U	E	E	K	T	C	E
F	G	O	O	D	H	T

☆ Hadith
☆ Scale
☆ Prophet
☆ Allah
☆ Yusuf
☆ Good

3- Which Prophet was put in prison and interpreted dreams?
Circle the correct answer

4- There is nothing heavier on scales than...
Complete the Hadith

Good Character

[Timidhi]

5- Quranic Arabic
Trace the Arabic word and join the dots

Sun

حَتَّىٰٓ إِذَا بَلَغَ مَطْلِعَ
ٱلشَّمْسِ وَجَدَهَا تَطْلُعُ
عَلَىٰ قَوْمٍ لَّمْ نَجْعَل
لَّهُم مِّن دُونِهَا سِتْرًا

[Verse : 90]

COMPETITION TIME!

Watch the 17th episode for the questions

Circle the correct answer

Each correct answer is worth 2 points, leaving you with a total score out of 6

Let's see if you can beat The Azharis!

Question	Answer (Circle the correct answer)		Score
1	Father	Mother	
2	Al Firdaws	Al Wasat	
3	Aasiyah رضي الله عنها	Khadijah رضي الله عنها	

TOTAL SCORE

THE AZHARI PAD

Watch episode 17 for the question

SURAH AL KAHF — PAGE 53 — EPISODE - 17

Yajuj and Majuj

Verse 94 - 96

1- Are Yajuj and Majuj good people?
   Colour the correct answer

2- Dhul Qarnayn took money for helping them.
   Follow the maze to the correct answer

3- What did the people ask Dhul Qarnayn to do?

Write the answer below

4- When something good happens to us we should say:

Break the code | Refer to the code breaker sheet

_ _ _ _ _ _ _ _ _ _ _ _

5- Quranic Arabic

Trace the Arabic word and join the dots

Nar

Fire

حَتَّىٰ إِذَا جَعَلَهُۥ نَارًا قَالَ
ءَاتُونِىٓ أُفْرِغْ عَلَيْهِ قِطْرًا

[Verse : 96]

COMPETITION TIME!

Watch the 18th episode for the questions

Circle the correct answer

Each correct answer is worth 2 points, leaving you with a total score out of 6

Let's see if you can beat The Azharis!

Question	Answer (Circle the correct answer)		Score
1	Adam عليه السلام	Nuh عليه السلام	
2	Musa عليه السلام	Eesa عليه السلام	
3	Ramadan	Muharram	
	TOTAL SCORE		

THE AZHARI PAD

Watch episode 18 for the question

SURAH AL KAHF — PAGE 56 — EPISODE - 18

End of Yajuj and Majuj

Verse 97 - 99

1- What did Dhul Qarnayn use to cover Yajuj & Majuj?
Join the dots

Iron and Copper

2- Yajuj & Majuj will drink all the water around them?
Circle the correct answer

True | False

SURAH AL KAHF   PAGE 57   EPISODE - 19

3- Which angel will blow the trumpet?

Colour in

عليه السلام

عليه السلام

عليه السلام

4- What will kill Yajuj & Majuj?

Break the code | Refer to the code breaker sheet

__ __ __ __ __

5- Quranic Arabic

Trace the Arabic word and join the dots

To come

قَالَ هَٰذَا رَحْمَةٌ مِّن رَّبِّى ۖ فَإِذَا جَآءَ وَعْدُ رَبِّى جَعَلَهُۥ دَكَّآءَ ۖ وَكَانَ وَعْدُ رَبِّى حَقًّا

[Verse : 98]

COMPETITION TIME!

Watch the 19th episode for the questions

Circle the correct answer

Each correct answer is worth 2 points, leaving you with a total score out of 6

Let's see if you can beat The Azharis!

Question	Answer		Score
	(Circle the correct answer)		
1	Surah Al Imran	Surah Al Baqarah	
2	One	Two	
3	Left	Right	
TOTAL SCORE			

THE AZHARI PAD

Watch episode 19 for the question

SURAH AL KAHF PAGE 59 EPISODE - 19

The Ka'bah

Verse 100 -110

DON'T FORGET!

Download your achievement certificate after completing 20 epsiodes from www.theazharis.com

1- How many angels will hold the throne of Allah?

Circle the correct answer

8   9   10

2- How long does it take to fly from their ear lobe to shoulder?

Find your way to the correct answer

START

700 years

700 days

SURAH AL KAHF   PAGE 60   EPISODE - 20

3- What is best place in Jannah?

Break the code | Refer to the code breaker sheet

___ ___ ___ ___ ___ ___ ___

4- What was the dua recited whilst building the Kabah?

Colour in

Rabbana taqabbal minna innaka antas sameeul aleem

[Surah Al-Baqarah : 127]

5- Quranic Arabic

Trace the Arabic word and join the dots

Qul

Say

قُل لَّوْ كَانَ ٱلْبَحْرُ مِدَادًا لِّكَلِمَٰتِ رَبِّى لَنَفِدَ ٱلْبَحْرُ قَبْلَ أَن تَنفَدَ كَلِمَٰتُ رَبِّى وَلَوْ جِئْنَا بِمِثْلِهِۦ مَدَدًا

[Verse : 109]

COMPETITION TIME!

Watch the 20th episode for the questions

Circle the correct answer

Each correct answer is worth 2 points, leaving you with a total score out of 6

Let's see if you can beat The Azharis!

Question	Answer (Circle the correct answer)		Score
1	63	93	
2	Left	Right	
3	True	False	
TOTAL SCORE			

THE AZHARI PAD

Watch episode 20 for the question

SURAH AL KAHF

Glossary

ARABIC WORD	TRANSLITERATION	MEANING	VERSE NO.
الْحَمْدُ لِلّه	Alhamdulillah	All praise belongs to Allah	1
أَجْر	Ajr	Reward	2
أَرْض	Ard	Earth	7
قَلْب	Qalb	Heart	14
رَحْمَة	Rahma	Mercy	16
صَبْر	Sabr	Patience	28
ثَمَر	Thamar	Fruit	34
مَال	Maal	Money	39
حَقّ	Haq	Truth	44
أَنْزَل	Anzal	To Decend	45
نَاس	Nas	People	54
يَد	Yad	Hand	57
نَسِيَ	Nasiya	To Forget	63
سَفِينَة	Safeenah	Boat	71
مَلِك	Malik	King	79
خَيْر	Khair	Good	81
شَمْس	Shams	Sun	90
نَار	Nar	Fire	96
جَاءَ	Jaa-a	To Come	98
قُلْ	Qul	Say	109

Answers

EPISODE - 1
1- Mecca
2- 10
3- Regularly
4- —

EPISODE - 2
1- Jannah
2- True
3- Slave
4- —

EPISODE - 3
1- Yes
2- Making Dua
3- Yes
4- Ihsan

EPISODE - 4
1- Ear
2- 309
3- Escape the people worshipping idols
4- To Others

EPISODE - 5
1- Allah turned them
2- Treasure
3- Healthy
4- —

EPISODE - 6
1- Dog
2- —
3- Four
4- 7

EPISODE - 7
1- Both
2- Thanking Allah
3- —
4- —

EPISODE - 8
1- Short Time
2- Earth
3- Masha Allah
4- False

EPISODE - 9
1- No
2- —
3- Intention
4- Destroyed

EPISODE - 10
1- Rain
2- Subhanallah, Alhamdulillah Allahu Akbar
3- Right
4- True

EPISODE - 11
1- No
2- 70,000
3- —
4- —

EPISODE - 12
1- False
2- Yusha
3- Ask for forgiveness
4- Fish

EPISODE - 13
1- Yusha
2- —
3- Khidr
4- Green

EPISODE - 14
1- Patience
2- InshaAllah
3- Boat
4- Not to ask questions

EPISODE - 15
1- Dawud
2- It was damaged
3- No
4- Rebuild It

EPISODE - 16
1- Orphans
2- A person with 2 horns
3- Treasure
4- —

EPISODE - 17
1- Yes
2- —
3- Yusuf عليه السلام
4- Good Character

EPISODE - 18
1- No
2- No
3- Build a barrier
4- Alhamdulillah

EPISODE - 19
1- Iron and Copper
2- True
3- Israfil عليه السلام
4- Worms

EPISODE - 20
1- 8
2- 700 years
3- Firdaws
4- —

THE AZHARIS

ALSO IN THE SERIES:

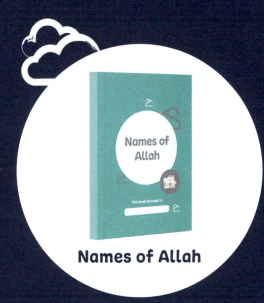

Names of Allah

Juz by Juz Stories

Who is Allah

www.theazharis.com

السَّلَامُ عَلَيْكُمْ وَرَحْمَةُ اللهِ وَبَرَكَاتُهُ

InshaAllah we hope that this series brings you closer to the Qur'an and that Allah enables us to be amongst those closest to Him, the people of the Qur'an and to recite Surah Al Kahf every Friday.

إِنَّ لِلَّهِ أَهْلِينَ مِنْ النَّاسِ
قَالُوا يَا رَسُولَ اللَّهِ مَنْ هُمْ
قَالَ هُمْ أَهْلُ الْقُرْآنِ

"Indeed, Allah has His own people among humanity." They said, "Oh Messenger of Allah, who are they?" The Prophet ﷺ said, "They are the people of the Quran."

- IBN MAJAH -

Sheikh Dr. Saalim Al-Azhari